*Passing over the bridge at Lowther Castle, Cumbria, are the Welsh cobs Venture and Viking, driven to a 'T' cart by Mrs Christine Dick. The next pair are grey Hungarians, Khaland and Bujan, driven to a Bennington phaeton by Mr S. V. Kaltenborn.*

# THE HARNESS HORSE

## Edward and Audrey Hart

## Shire Publications Ltd

G000065959

# CONTENTS

Published in 1994 by Shire Publications Ltd, Cromwell House, Church Street, Princes Risborough, Buckinghamshire HP27 9AA, UK.
Copyright © 1994 by Edward and Audrey Hart. First published 1981; reprinted 1986. Second edition 1994. Shire Album 53. ISBN 0 7478 0246 7.

All rights reserved. No part of this publication may be reproduced or transmitted in any form or by any means, electronic or mechanical, including photocopy, recording, or any information storage and retrieval system, without permission in writing from the publishers.

Printed in Great Britain by CIT Printing Services, Press Buildings, Merlins Bridge, Haverfordwest, Dyfed SA61 1XF.

British Library Cataloguing in Publication Data: Hart, Edward and Audrey. Harness Horse. 2 Rev. ed. – (Shire Albums; No. 53). I. Title. II. Series. 798. 6. ISBN 0-7478-0246-7.

## ACKNOWLEDGEMENTS

The authors express their thanks to Mrs Phyllis Candler of the British Driving Society, to the British Horse Society, and to Thomas Fawcett for reading the proofs. The second edition owes much to Arthur and Gwynne Floyd, to Ted Hall, and to Stella Havard for information on harness racing.

The cover photograph is by Graham and Barbara Swanson. Other photographs are acknowledged as follows: Michael Bass, Reed Photography, page 9; *Evening Sentinel* (Stoke-on-Trent), pages 2, 32; Gwynne Floyd, pages 3, 30; Audrey Hart, pages 1, 4, 5, 6, 7, 10 (both), 11 (both), 14 (bottom), 15, 16, 20 (top), 23, 25, 26 (both), 28; Edward Hart, pages 8, 22 (bottom), 24; Don Kelly, page 18; Cadbury Lamb, pages 17, 19, 20 (bottom), 21 (both), 22 (top); Tir Prince Raceway, page 27; *Your Horse*, page 14 (top).

Cover: *A sociable being driven past the Royal Crescent, Bath.*

Below: *Bess driven to a home-built modern gig, copied from the old Stanhope spindle-backed gig. Bess is a pedigree Welsh cob, bred at Moffat in southern Scotland, and stands 15.2 hands high. She has three different sizes of collar; her neck width varies throughout the year. She is also broken to ride.*

*A lady's phaeton with a 13.2 hands dun pony. This four-wheeled vehicle was designed to be driven by a groom, with a low step for the lady to alight easily. She must be dressed in ladylike fashion.*

# INTRODUCTION

Arthur Young wrote of a waterlogged England during his late eighteenth-century tours. As not even the fields were drained, the tracks between them that served as roads were unimaginably wet and rutted. This necessitated very strong vehicles and heavy horses to pull them. Not until Macadam improved Britain's roads did driving in its modern form become possible.

The years 1820 to 1840 were the golden age of coaching. The roads were passable at speed and the railways had not arrived. The Royal Mail coach was king of the road. It could average up to 11 miles (18 km) per hour and other vehicles were expected to make way for it. The stage-coach carried an armed guard with his 'yard of tin' posthorn, with which he gave advance warning of its approach. Postboys were wiry fellows who drove the coach from the saddle of the nearside wheeler. Horses were changed at posting houses along the route, every 15 miles (24 km) or so, so that the coach could travel at speed. Travelling post cost 1s 6d a mile.

When the railways arrived, the large vehicles for carrying passengers and luggage over long distances began to disappear, but horse transport remained essential for local journeys and the development of types of light carriage continued into the twentieth century. Those sporting vehicles that had been popular since the late eighteenth century were outnumbered by more sedate types put to uses as diverse as taking the air in the park, transporting dogs and delivering groceries.

Interest in the harness horse has grown gradually since the 1950s, but in the early years after the Second World War it appeared that the road horse had indeed gone for ever. Driving then became a sport, with more and more classes at local and regional shows. It has gained further impetus through the interest and skill of the Duke of Edinburgh with his team of four Cleveland Bays. The Queen opens Smith's Lawn, Windsor, each June for a driving rally that includes singles, pairs, tandems, unicorns and four-in-hands, besides governess carts and a *concours d'elegance*. There is great pleasure in driving and owning gracious vehicles and well-schooled horses, and no other sport offers a more interesting, agreeable and nostalgic spectacle.

3

*A useful ride-and-drive type of animal with enough bone for a considerable load, this cob is driven to a gig. Note the very light wheels and the breast collar.*

*Norwegian Fjord ponies driven to a Lawton phaeton. Phaetons are carriages on four wheels, generally carrying four people. A large number of different types of phaeton exist. They include basket, Beaufort, cab, cabriolet, crane-neck, demi-mail, dogcart, drop-front, equirotal, George IV, mail, Malvern, park, Parisian, perch-high, pony, queen, Siamese, spider, Stanhope, 'T' cart and tub phaetons.*

# BREEDS

Any type of horse which pulls a vehicle does so by means of harness, but the generally accepted definition of a 'harness horse' is one of the lighter breeds that moves readily at the trot and not the heavy Clydesdale, Percheron, Shire and Suffolk, whose weight may approach a ton and whose natural gait is the walk. Because of differences in the size, strength, action and temperament of the various breeds they are used with different types of vehicle. They range from the small Shetland pony to the tall Cleveland Bay and Gelderlander.

*Shetland ponies* are perhaps the most popular of British breeds. Small and thick-set, with large lively eyes, they are extremely strong, hardy, friendly and biddable and they can subsist on a very sparse diet. Most commonly black or dark brown, they can be any colour. As harness ponies they have been popular since the nineteenth century, when the breed quality was improved to produce sound animals to work in the mines.

The *Dartmoor pony* typifies the best pony characteristics. Up to 12.2 hands high, but usually smaller, he has a small intelligent head with prick ears, medium-length neck, deep girth, flowing mane, forelock and tail and muscular hindquarters. Outcrossing with Arabs and Thoroughbreds helped refine the form of the Dartmoor pony, which is usually black, brown or bay and may not be piebald or skewbald.

*Exmoor ponies* share common ancestors with the Dartmoor but today they are bigger and more rugged and their heavy-lidded (toad) eyes, mealy-coloured noses and double-textured coats are distinctive. In colour they may be bay, brown or grey dun. They are extremely strong and need firm handling. They have been harness ponies for generations above and below ground.

*Welsh ponies* are divided into four sections, the smallest being section A, the Welsh Mountain pony, not exceeding 12 hands. Section B is of popular riding height, the limit being 13.2 hands, but sprightly in harness. Section C has a similar height limit but is rather stronger and highly regarded as a driving pony. The Welsh may be any colour except piebald and skewbald. Seen at their best at the Royal Welsh Show near Builth Wells in June, they offer the widest of choices to the driving enthusiast.

*Welsh cobs,* section D, are very popular ride-and-drive animals, having been bred as cobs for all purposes on the farm. Although cobs may be up to 15.2 hands high they must be of pony type and not small horses. High-spirited, with a distinctive trotting action and great stamina, the Welsh cob excels in harness. They should look like larger versions of the Welsh Mountain pony from which they derive.

The *Highland pony* is becoming more popular in harness as it is steady and untemperamental, qualities encouraged by continuous use on the farm and for stalking, shooting and trekking. It is a large solid pony, up to 14.2 hands in height, and has a variety of attractive colours, often

*The collecting ring at the Lowther Trials, Cumbria. Major driving events are a good place to study the wide range of vehicles and horses. Nearest the camera is a phaeton with its four-in-hand team of Exmoor ponies. The phaeton is an ideal family vehicle, much used in Victorian times for visiting. It may be for one horse or two, and it has easy access and folding seats for luggage.*

*The Queen's team of fine Cleveland Bays, driven to a dogcart by the Duke of Edinburgh. The Duke has given much impetus to competitive driving and says that, unlike in polo, the horses do most of the work.*

enhanced by silver manes and tails. Along the back runs a black eel stripe and there are often dark stripes on the forelegs.

Deliberate breeding policy from 1924 helped restore the *Connemara* as a true breed. The commonest colour is grey, but black, bay brown and dun are seen, with the occasional roan or chestnut. Allowed up to 14 hands, the pony is short-legged with sloping shoulders and a deep body. Usually hardy, good-tempered and intelligent, the Connemara is ideal for riding or driving.

*New Forest ponies* vary in type, not least because of the introduction in the nineteenth century of other native breeds to improve a breed declining in quality. Usually well made, and standing up to 14.2 hands, with comparatively short necks and large heads, they have good short legs and may be any colour but piebald or skewbald. Constant contact with humans has made them docile and they are intelligent and versatile.

*Fell* and *Dales ponies* have emerged as separate types since the late nineteenth century, and the Fell pony looks like a smaller version of the Dales. Predominantly black or brown, they are genuine working ponies and ideal for trekking and driving. They are not inclined to canter or gallop very far but can set out at a smart trot and are almost tireless. The Dales is allowed 14.2 hands, the Fell 14 hands.

The *Cleveland Bay* is a handsome horse of an old breed from north-east Yorkshire that used to be packhorses. It is strongly built with a long neck, large convex head, very deep girth and strong short legs. Usually bay with a black mane and tail, it stands up to 16.2 hands and is intelligent with great stamina and an excellent harness horse.

The most spectacular horse is undoubtedly the *Hackney*. Standing up to 16 hands, with head held high on a graceful curved neck, its elegant lines are matched by its unique elevated trotting action, in which each foot seems to spring off the ground. Usually bay, brown, black or chestnut, often with white markings, it is the supreme harness horse of the showring. The descendant of native trotting mares, Arabs and Thoroughbreds, it is strong, intelligent and docile.

The black *Friesian* horse carries a long fine head high above a muscular body on short but powerful legs. Sensitive, pleasant and hard working, it is very active with a good trotting action and is used in the circus as well as for driving.

The *Appaloosa*, too is a circus horse, immediately identifiable by its spots and striped hooves. It is usually roan but the spots vary in colour and formation. In harness it is very versatile, active and dependable.

Like the Highland pony, the *Norwegian Fjord pony* bears a dorsal stripe and black stripes on the forelegs. It is found in all shades of dun, but particularly an attractive creamy colour. The stripe is often emphasised by clipping the mane so that the black shows through. The Fjord pony is tough, sturdy and well-shaped, standing up to 14.2 hands, and very good in harness.

Commonly chestnut or grey, the *Gelderland* horse is a typical carriage horse, standing up to 17 hands, with short strong legs. It probably owes its good movement to crossing with Norfolk Roadsters and it is docile and manoeuvrable.

*Harness horses must back as well as pull forwards. These Gelderlanders have been delivering beer in the streets of Sunderland.*

*A beautiful pair of greys. The rein on the right of the photograph is looped below the ring, indicating the need for more pressure. The other horse is driven satisfactorily with the rein through the ring, giving the lightest pressure.*

# HARNESS

The purpose of harness is to link the horse to the vehicle so as to make efficient and safe use of the horse's pulling power. The horse applies its power through the *collar*, of which there are two main types, neck and breast. The leather *neck collar* rests on the horse's shoulders and should fit snugly without any seesaw motion. The closed-top collar is complete in itself, while the open-top has two peaks, the two sides being kept together at the top by the cape (or housing) and housing strap and buckle, strapped as tight as possible. Though many other natural and synthetic materials have been tried as padding for the collar, tightly packed wheat or rye straw remains the most serviceable.

The front of the collar is framed by the metal *hames*, joined above and below by adjustable tightening straps. The hames help to maintain or adjust the shape of the collar, but their principal function is to carry on each side hame tugs to which are attached the long leather traces to connect the horse with the vehicle. At the vehicle end the traces are joined either to *shaft hooks* or to a *swingletree*. The latter insulates the direct pull and is more comfortable for the horse. The hames also carry a loop at each side through which the reins pass. For harnessing to a central pole there is a loop at the bottom of the hames to which the supporting chain or straps are attached.

Above: *The light cart is most useful for any large garden or smallholding. Here a neighbour's piebald pony, Patch, is being used by the author to move a midden. Patch is a useful ride-and-drive animal that will go anywhere and do anything. Such ponies are comparatively cheap to keep, as their few hours of work a week do not call for heavy concentrate feeding.*

Left: *The breeching, or leather webbing enabling the horse to back a load or prevent it running forward if going downhill. The breeching is connected to the shafts by a breechings chain or by a strap as used here. Shafts are normally of ash wood.*

10

*The light saddle or pad (centre) supports the shafts and provides safe anchorage for the brass rings used to keep the reins at a convenient height. Reins should run in as straight a line as possible from the horse's mouth to the hands of the driver. The ring attached by a short chain to the top of the hames assists this and helps prevent the reins from dropping down and becoming entangled.*

*Attachment of the tug chain to the hames (extreme right). There are many ways of harnessing but this is a simple and well-tried method for a light cart. The hames are of metal or wood and detach from the collar by means of a strap (as here) or short chain at the base of the collar, and a hame strap at the top. The collar must fit snugly, or sore shoulders will result. A plough line is used, but leather reins are necessary for smartness.*

11

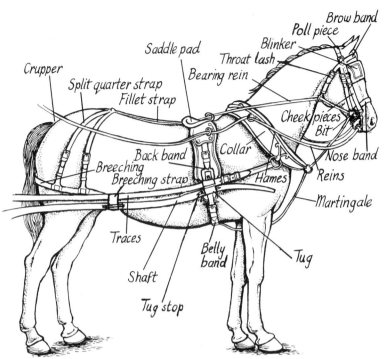

*The principal parts of the harness.*

The *breast collar* is a broad strap of leather, usually padded with felt, which passes round the horse's breast and is supported by a strap over the neck. The traces are attached at the shoulders. It is not so efficient as a neck collar because the horse cannot exert so much pull, but it is cooler, cheaper and more easily cut in case of accident, and it can be adjusted to fit another animal in a few minutes. It was used a great deal by the army and today Hackneys are frequently shown in a breast strap.

The harness horse pulls his load through his collar, in the direction indicated by his driver through the *bridle*, which is a framework of straps around his head culminating in a *bit*, which passes through his mouth. The driving reins are attached to a ring at either end of the bit.

Common driving bits include the Liverpool, the traditional driving bit with straight bar. Wilson's traditional trade bit comprises a snaffle or jointed bit with four rings to allow varying degrees of leverage. The Buxton is the Liverpool with a bar underneath, used for tandems and pairs (to stop them eating each other!).

The parts of the bridle are the *poll piece*, fitting behind the ears; the *browband* in front of the ears, sometimes decorated; the *cheek piece*, from the junction of the browband and the poll piece to the bit; the *noseband*, joining the two cheek pieces clear of the nostrils; the *blinkers*, solid pieces of leather which prevent the animal seeing sideways or backwards without turning his head; and the *throat lash*. This passes under the jowl and must not be too tight or it interferes with breathing.

The shafts or pole are supported by the *harness saddle*, placed well forward on the back of the horse. It consists of two leather panels, joined at the top, over a wooden saddle tree which is covered and padded. Each panel bears a *shaft tug* through which the shaft passes. The saddle is secured by the *backband*, which passes through it and buckles on to the *bellyband*, and behind by the *crupper*, which loops under the tail root. Where there are no shafts to carry, as in four-in-hand teams, a light *driving pad* is used. There are metal loops on top for the reins to pass through.

To enable the horse to stop a brakeless vehicle, a *breeching* is fitted round the animal's haunches, consisting of a broad leather strap, attached at each side to the shafts, supported by one or two straps over the back connecting with the crupper. By leaning backwards into the strap, the horse can slow down, stop and ultimately reverse the vehicle.

In driving, the whip is carried in the right hand. The *reins* should be held in the left hand, the right hand being used on occasion to draw them up and shorten them. The two reins should be held one between the thumb and first finger and the other between the middle and third fingers. When driving a four-horse team, the near lead rein (to the leading horse on the driver's left) is held over the left forefinger. The off lead rein (to the right-hand front horse) is held between the fore and middle fingers, the near wheel rein (to the left-hand horse nearest the driver) is held under the off lead, and the off wheel rein between the middle and third fingers. When driving, the two hands should never be used equally as they are when riding a horse, although there is a growing tendency to do so, even among top performers. The whip should be as light as possible and well balanced, with the thong about half the length of the stick. Its purpose is to remind horses rather than to chastise them. A whip needs care to prevent warping and should always be hung on a special whip reel when not in use.

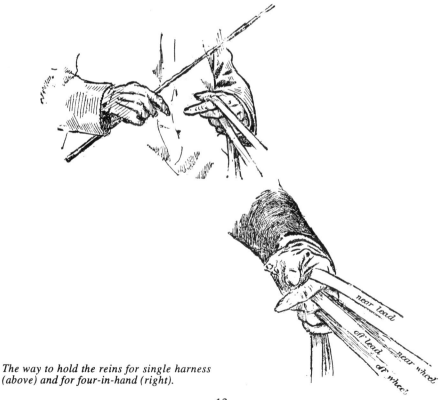

*The way to hold the reins for single harness (above) and for four-in-hand (right).*

13

*Susie, a 13.2 hands pony, is exercising in a collar. A swingletree links the traces to the vehicle. It helps take friction away from the shoulders and lessens the sideways sway of the vehicle as each foreleg advances in turn.*

*The two-wheeled dogcart, drawn by cobs Jack and Jill. A dogcart takes four people and varies in height. Its balance is arranged by screw or lever, or simply by moving the seats.*

*The lady on the left is driving a pair of Irish hunters using breast collars. The vehicle is a continental wagonette. On the right are Irish/Arab ponies driven to a Bennington dogcart. Originally used for carting gundogs to shoots, dogcarts have large underboots fitted with ventilation slits.*

# VEHICLES

Many of the vehicles driven in showing classes are originals which had a working life before they were ousted by the motor-car. A few have been in continuous use. But as driving has become more popular the demand for originals has outstripped supply and more new vehicles, some reproductions, others made for competition, are appearing every year. The variety of vehicles entering a combined driving event is part of its charm. Teams of four horses are driven to anything from a demi-mail phaeton to a wagonette, a Hamshaw brake or a Bristow battlewagon. In the pairs classes, the range of vehicles is even greater. A modern dogcart, a Bennington competition vehicle, a phaeton or a 'T' cart are hauled by the bigger horses, while pairs of ponies are driven to traps, dogcarts, Lawton phaetons or Danish dogcarts. In the single harness classes, many types of gig are found, as are Norfolk carts, ralli cars or cross-country vehicles. Though the novice spectator may feel bemused by the different types, they soon fit into their categories.

In one-, two- and three-day competition events, special vehicles are used for cross-country sections. They are mostly modern, using mainly metal construction with low centre of gravity. Popular makes include Bellcrown, Bennington, Fenix, Kilbride, Jacksons and many others.

*A Norfolk cart and skewbald Welsh-cross pony with breast collar.*

## FASHIONABLE CARRIAGES OF 1888

| Name of carriage | Size of horse | Number of persons carried |
|---|---|---|
| **Two-wheelers** | | |
| Pony cart | 1 pony, 12 to 14 hands | 2 |
| Dogcart | 1 horse, $14^1/2$ to 16 hands | 4 |
| Gig | 1 horse, $15^1/2$ hands | 2 |
| Hansom cab | 1 horse, 16 hands | 3 (2 inside, driver behind) |
| | | |
| **Four-wheelers** | | |
| Phaeton | 1 horse, 15 hands | 4 |
| Road phaeton | 1 horse, $15^1/2$ hands | 4 (2 in front, 2 behind) |
| 'T' cart | 1 horse, $15^1/2$ hands | 4 (2 in front, 2 behind) |
| Park phaeton | 2 horses, from 15 hands | 3 (2 in front, 1 behind) |
| Victoria | 1 or 2 horses, $15^1/2$ hands | 4 or 6 (2 in front, 2 or 4 inside) |
| Double victoria | 2 horses, $15^1/2$ hands | 6 (4 inside, 2 in front) |
| Stanhope phaeton | 2 horses, 16 hands | 4 (2 in front, 2 behind) |
| Mail phaeton | 2 or 4 horses, 16 hands | 4 (2 in front, 2 behind) |
| Pair-horse wagonette | 2 horses, 16 hands | 6 (4 behind, 2 in front) |
| Pair-horse brake | 2 horses, 16 hands | 8 (6 behind, 2 in front) |

*Rear view of a gig. One important difference between a trap and a gig is that on a trap the seat moves but on a modern gig the body moves.*

*The coloured cob Dinah – note the white on the withers – drawing a ralli car made in 1910. The passengers enter first and sit in the back. The front seat slides back and forth to give balance once the driver and groom are seated.*

| *Name of carriage* | *Size of horse* | *Number of persons carried* |
| --- | --- | --- |
| Pair-horse omnibus | 2 horses, 16 hands | |
| Miniature brougham | 1 horse, 15.2 hands | 4 (2 inside, 2 in front) |
| Single brougham | 1 horse, 15.2 hands | 4 (2 inside, 2 in front) |
| Circular-fronted brougham | 1 horse, 15.2 hands | 6 (4 inside, 2 in front) |
| Double brougham | 1 or 2 horses, 15.2 hands | 6 (4 inside, 2 in front) |
| Single brougham on under and 'C' springs | 1 horse, 15.2 hands | 4 (2 inside, 2 in front) |
| Double brougham on under and 'C' springs | 2 horses, 15.2 hands | 6 (4 inside, 2 in front) |
| Sociable | 2 horses, 15 hands | 6 (4 inside, 2 in front) |
| Barouche-sociable | 2 horses, 15$^1$/2 hands | 6 (4 inside, 2 in front) |
| Barouche on elliptical springs | 2 horses, 15$^1$/2 hands | 6 (4 inside, 2 in front) |
| Barouche on under and 'C' springs | 2 horses, 15$^1$/2 hands | 6 (4 inside, 2 in front) |
| Light coach on elliptical springs | 2 horses, 15 hands | 6 (4 inside, 2 in front) |
| Light coach on under and 'C' springs | 2 horses, 15$^1$/2 hands | 6 (4 inside, 2 in front) |
| Shelburne landau | 2 horses, 15$^1$/2 hands | 6 (4 inside, 2 in front) |
| Sefton landau | 2 horses, 15$^1$/2 hands | 6 (4 inside, 2 in front) |
| Landau on under and 'C' springs | 2 horses, 16 hands | 6 (4 inside, 2 in front) |
| Dress chariot | 2 horses, 16 hands | 3 (2 inside, 1 in front) |
| Dress coach | 2 horses, 16 hands | 5 (4 inside, 1 in front) |
| Four-in-hand drag | 4 horses, 16 hands | 14 |

## LIGHT TRADE

A universally popular class at any country show is Light Trade. It is for trade vehicles of a type lighter than those requiring an accepted heavy breed, such as Shire or Clydesdale. Light Trade embraces both delivery and passenger vehicles – wagonettes or even hansom cabs – but not the type that would appear under Private Driving. It could include anything from a rag and bone man's flat cart to a smart butcher's delivery cart. The Bradford flat cart may be very ornate, with intricate carving on front and rear, artistically painted.

A Light Trade vehicle is horsed by anything from a quite small pony to a 'vanner'. This very useful animal usually has some hair on its legs, is probably derived from the Shire or Clydesdale one or two generations back, but is active enough to perform its work at a good working trot when necessary.

The British Driving Society issues useful guidelines, written by Norman Robarts. They include:

'Is the horse able to pull the load adequately? Will it stand unattended if required? Trade horses should walk quietly and sensibly, as well as trot. Light Trade horses should be able to back at least five yards, preferably ten. Trade harness should be black, and not too flashy. Fittings should match those on the vehicle. It is important to consider the ability of the animal for the job. I would expect a good sharp goer in a baker's cart, butcher's cart or milk float, because in the days when they were in use the average daily journey could have been 12 to 20 miles.'

Coster vehicles are a form of Light Trade, but by definition they must carry goods sold from the vehicles themselves. Classes are found mainly in London and the Home Counties, and among the best places to see costers are the London Harness Parade and the Royal International Horse Show.

*A sturdy pony with a rulley to match. Such vehicles are very useful for the delivery of sacks.*

*This roan Welsh cob is driven to a cut-under gig, a sporting vehicle giving clear views of the countryside. One of the joys of driving is that the pace is ideal for 'looking over the hedge'. The carriage lamps fitted here are very scarce, so many having been used to light driveways.*

*The milk float is among the most familiar conveyances. The pony can be trained to move on command to the next stop and knows its route as well as the driver.*

*The four-wheeled dogcart was originally designed, as its name suggests, to carry gundogs to the shooting field. It became a familiar general-purpose vehicle.*

*Two lovely greys harnessed to a phaeton. Phaetons diversified into a number of designs; the original was designed to seat two persons, including the driver, and ran on four wheels.*

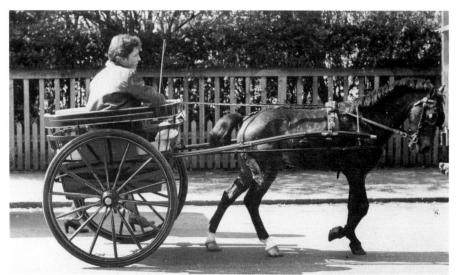

*A tub trap suitable for a very small pony. Note the tension on the leather trace and breast collar.*

*A game cart with racks for rabbits. The design ensures a free flow of air.*

*A Bennington competition vehicle drawn by four Welsh cobs. The crowd on the embankment shows the great interest in driving. Ideally, teams are matched for colour, but they must also be similar in pace and temperament. A light-coloured horse with three dark ones makes an attractive combination.*

# COMPETITIONS

Combined driving competitions fall under three main headings: dressage, the marathon and the obstacle course. The dressage test is designed to judge the freedom, regularity of pace and ease of movement of the horses, combined with harmony, impulsion, suppleness, lightness and correct positioning of the horse or horses on the move. Each driver is judged on his style, accuracy and command of the team. The test may be combined with presentation, when the judge notes the turn-out, cleanliness and general condition and impression of the horses or ponies. Driver, grooms, harness and vehicle also come under close scrutiny.

A typical advanced dressage test entails entering the arena at a collected trot, halting and saluting. The team then moves at a working trot in a half circle right, followed by a half circle left. After driving diagonally across the arena, a complete circle is made, followed by another diagonal and circle. A serpentine of five loops gives way to a walk and then a halt of ten seconds. The team is reined back and circled several times before making a final halt and salute. Spectators will find details in the catalogues at each event.

The marathon is a drive out in the country to test the fitness and stamina of the horses and the judgement of pace and horsemanship of their drivers. No precise distance is laid down, but 8 miles (13 km) is common. The course is divided into sections, some being completed at the trot, others at the walk only. Natural or artificial obstacles such as gates, sharp turns, water and steep hills add to the variety. The water crossing is especially popular with spectators, who watch each team approach the fordable river at a trot, brave

*The river crossing is a popular part of the marathon with the spectators. Fordable streams are a first-class test for horses and drivers. Here a modern competition vehicle is used, the team being Welsh cobs.*

the running waters and emerge splashing up the far bank with little change in their vehicle's pace.

A referee travels with each team. In addition to timing the journey, he notes any adjustment of harness, any un-coachmanlike action on the part of the coachman when passing other coaches, whether a stop was made to rub down horses or harness (not allowed), and the number of persons carried.

In the obstacle test, teams negotiate a series of narrow 'gates', consisting of markers of the type used for road diversions. These are set at varying widths and difficult angles and, as time usually counts in such events, there is the temptation to take the obstacle at speed. With a pony and trap this is difficult enough; when a spirited four-in-hand is being driven, slight pressure on the bit is necessary to avoid losing points through striking the obstacle. Such events are great fun for the spectator, and the scurry driving at the Horse of the Year Show at Wembley each October is invariably a highlight.

TANDEM DRIVING

Tandem driving has been described as 'using two horses to do the work of one'.

This style of driving has the considerable disadvantage that the lead horse is on his own, with no companion to keep him straight, and he is too far from the coachman to be completely controlled by him.

Driving two horses, one in front of the other, is a difficult art and mishaps quickly occur if the leader takes it into his head to swing round, into the horse and harness behind him. The coachman may have no alternative but to follow round with the wheeler and then set off on the correct course after another turn.

The leader must be bold and free. He must ignore all other traffic and be well accustomed to single harness. When the team is going well it makes a fine sight, and, with all the traces taut, up a slight incline the extra horse is a big advantage. Downhill, much skill is needed to prevent him either stepping over the traces or pulling on too fast.

PRIVATE DRIVING

Private Driving classes provide some of the most stylish and spectacular scenes in the summer show season. In origin they were non-competitive; this form of driving was simply what people did themselves for relaxation in their parks. It is

24

*A minimum number of persons must be carried throughout the marathon. The groom's function is important: he or she must be ready at all times for an emergency and to hold the horses' heads during an enforced stop. This groom is having a lift to the stables, not a legal position for the marathon or at any other times.*

Tandem driving. The lead horse is a New Forest cross, and the shaft horse a skewbald, driven to a ralli car. These vehicles effectively replace older types. The leather traces of the lead horse should be taut; he is there to work, not merely for show.

The gallop is not a recommended pace in modern driving, and these Welsh ponies are behaving rather exuberantly. Only two of the sixteen feet are on the ground! The vehicle is a dogcart.

fundamentally different from carriage driving in that no coachman is employed. Driving is usually from the body of the vehicle, and neither driver nor groom is ever in livery.

Though there is no limit to the number of horses, a single or a pair is most usual.

Most county and many country shows now stage Private Driving classes. It is judged on manners, fit of harness, suitability of vehicle and cleanliness, and smartness of driver and groom. But, as one judge remarked, there is no point in dressing up to the nines if the horse misbehaves!

## HARNESS RACING

Though the sport of harness racing is very popular in the USA and is widespread on the European mainland, in Britain it has never compared with flat racing for popularity. It is well established in Cumbria and North Wales, with strong centres of interest around York and Birmingham.

Harness racing is usually conducted in heats of four, often on a hard track, sometimes on grass. The horses draw a very light sulky, weighing only about 40 pounds (18 kg), with bicycle-type wheels and little else but a frame, a seat and a pair of light shafts.

Tracks are generally half a mile (800 metres) or a quarter of a mile (400 metres), though the track at the Kendal racecourse, Cumbria, is 660 yards (600 metres).

The horse used is the Standardbred, which has its own studbook. It is derived from Thoroughbred and Arab blood, and there has been much interchange of blood between countries in recent years. The Standardbred may be any colour and is generally over 15 hands.

Just as the Thoroughbred is the fastest ridden horse, so is the Standardbred the swiftest in harness. Its name is derived from the original nineteenth-century American harness studbooks, whose criterion for acceptance was to cover a mile in 'standard time'. That was initially 2 minutes 30 seconds; the 'two minute mile'

*Harness racing. The hobbles clearly seen on the flanks encourage the horses to 'pace', or use both legs on the same side together. The sport is very popular in many countries and is growing fast in Britain.*

*Chestnut Welsh cobs driven to a modern ralli car. When driving a tandem the right hand must be used frequently, to check any tendency on the leader's part to cross the road or turn a corner. Sceptics describe tandem driving as 'using two horses to do the work of one', but it is an interesting experience, given a well-matched team.*

barrier was broken in Britain in 1992, showing the rate of progress.

Though Standardbreds come in all colours, bays predominate, with a sprinkling of chestnuts and blacks but few greys or broken colours. Height averages 15 to 15.2 hands but ranges from 14 to 17 hands. Though tough and less prone to injury than Thoroughbreds, the world's fastest Standardbred racing stock traces back to an English Thoroughbred stallion, Messenger. Some American blood is used in Britain, and Europe and Australasia also stage harness racing.

There are two distinct gaits, pacing and trotting. Pacing is a 'lateral' gait in which the legs on the same side move back and forward together. This gait, natural to some horses, is encouraged by hobbles or straps connecting the legs on the same side.

Pacing or 'ambling' is faster than trotting by about three seconds per mile. Pacers are also less likely to 'break' or deviate from the proper pacing or trotting gait, and they dominate harness racing in the English-speaking world.

Trotting is a 'diagonal' gait in which the left fore and right hind legs move together almost simultaneously, followed by the right fore and left hind legs. Most horses trot naturally, and this gait is the only one recognised in Europe.

Standardbreds race in a sulky, a cart or 'bike' in which the driver sits with his legs along the shafts. With a well-balanced sulky the driver's weight makes little difference. Horses are handicapped according to the number of races they have won.

A new harness-racing track opened at Dunstall Park, Wolverhampton, in 1994. It is purpose-built inside the flat-racing course and will stage most of the harness-racing classics.

Other hard tracks are at Tir Prince, near Towyn, North Wales; York; Corbiewood, near Stirling; and Amman Valley, South Wales. There are also over forty grass circuits staging exciting summer evening meetings.

The sport's governing body is the British Harness Racing Club. It registers some 5000 trainers and drivers, many of them 'permit' trainers who own and drive their own horses. A similar number of horses is registered.

A horse may begin to race in non-betting qualifiers as a two-year-old, usually reaching its peak between three and six years old, though Dark Rhapsody was still winning at 21.

The United Kingdom mile record is held by Golden Dale and Alan Hawthornthwaite in 1 minute 59.4 seconds, set at York in June 1992.

There is no way of picking a winner on looks. Breeders with a lifetime's experience still have to test every one against the clock. Thus there are no in-hand classes for Standardbreds; speed is the only criterion. For thrilling, open-air sport amid convivial company, harness racing is hard to beat.

# DRIVING ORGANISATIONS

Driving in Britain is organised by the British Driving Society and the British Horse Society. The Combined Driving Group is a discipline of the latter. The British Driving Society arranges non-competitive rallies and instructional days through its system of Area Commissioners and has a panel of judges, lecturers and instructors. Driving classes at shows are affiliated to the British Driving Society, and the climax of the showing year is the Society's annual show, held at Windsor by kind permission of the Queen. There is also a Scottish branch of the Society.

The Combined Driving Group covers competitive one-day, two-day and three-day events and has the responsibility for funding driving teams going abroad to represent Britain.

The Hackney Horse Society is the governing body of Hackney driving, and its annual show is held at the South of England Showground at Ardingly, West Sussex, in June.

## HORSE DRIVING TRIALS

The principal events in the trials calendar include:

*April*: Thoresby Park, Nottingham.
*May*: Brighton, East Sussex; Windsor CAI, Royal Windsor Horse Show; St Fort, Newport-on-Tay, Fife.
*June*: Castle Howard, North Yorkshire; Tatton Park, Cheshire; Sandringham, Norfolk.
*July*: Drumlanrig Castle, Dumfries; Normanhurst, East Sussex; Streatlam Park, Durham; Exmoor, Somerset.

*Shandy, a Welsh section 'C' (Welsh pony of cob type), competing in Private Driving. The carriage lamp is obligatory in this section, and it must have a candle that has been lit. On a dark, wet night, lighting a previously unused candle is not easy.*

*August*: Lowther, Cumbria; Godmersham, Kent; Seacliff, East Lothian; Somerford, Cheshire.

*September*: National Championships, Windsor.

For further information contact the Horse Driving Trials Group: Manor Farm, Bascote, near Leamington Spa, Warwickshire CV33 0DX.

ADDRESSES

*British Driving Society*: Executive Secretary, Mrs J. Dillon, 27 Dugard Place, Barford, Warwick CV35 8DX. Telephone: 0926 624420.

*British Horse Society*: Chief Executive, Tim Eastwood, British Equestrian Centre, Stoneleigh Park, Kenilworth, Warwickshire CV8 2LR. Telephone: 0203 696697.

# PLACES TO VISIT

Intending visitors are advised to find out opening times and to check that relevant items are on display before travelling.

*Arlington Court*, Arlington, near Barnstaple, Devon EX31 4LP. Telephone: 0271 850296.

*Bass Museum, Visitor Centre and Shire Horse Stables*, Horninglow Street, Burton upon Trent, Staffordshire DE14 1JZ. Telephone: 0283 42031 or 511000.

*Beamish: The North of England Open Air Museum*, Beamish, County Durham DH9 0RG. Telephone: 0207 231811.

*Black Country Museum*, Tipton Road, Dudley, West Midlands DY1 4SQ. Telephone: 021-557 9643.

*Breamore Countryside Museum*, Breamore, Fordingbridge, Hampshire SP6 2DF. Telephone: 0725 22468.

*Brickfields Horsecountry*, Newnham Road, Binstead, near Ryde, Isle of Wight PO33 3TH. Telephone: 0983 66801.

*Bristol Industrial Museum*, Prince's Wharf, Prince Street, Bristol, Avon BS1 4RN. Telephone: 0272 251470.

*Buckland Abbey*, Yelverton, Devon PL20 6EY. Telephone: 0822 853607.

*Castle Howard*, near York YO6 7DA. Telephone: 0653 84333.

*Cockley Cley Iceni Village and Museums*, Cockley Cley, Swaffham, Norfolk PE37 8AG. Telephone: 0760 721339 or 24588.

*Cornish Shire Horse Trust and Carriage Museum*, Lower Gryllis, Treskillard, Redruth, Cornwall TR16 6LA. Telephone: 0209 713606.

*Courage Shire Horse Centre*, Cherry Garden Lane, Maidenhead Thicket, Maidenhead, Berkshire SL6 3QD. Telephone: 0628 824848.

*Gawsworth Hall*, Gawsworth, Macclesfield, Cheshire SK11 9RN. Telephone: 0260 223456.

*Glasgow Museum of Transport*, Kelvin Hall, 1 Bunhouse Road, Glasgow G3 8PZ. Telephone: 041-357 3929.

*Gunnersbury Park Museum*, Gunnersbury Park, London W3 8LQ. Telephone: 081-992 1612.

*Hampton Court Palace*, East Molesey, Surrey KT8 9AU. Telephone: 081-977 8441.

*Hereford and Worcester County Museum*, Hartlebury Castle, Hartlebury, near Kidderminster, Worcestershire DY11 7XZ. Telephone: 0299 250416.

*Jersey Shire Horse Centre*, Champ Donne, Route-de-Troupez, St Ouen, Jersey. Telephone: 0534 482372.

*London Transport Museum*, 39 Wellington Street, Covent Garden, London WC2E 7BB. Telephone: 071-379 6344.

*Manx Museum*, Douglas, Isle of Man. Telephone: 0624 675522.

*Museum of East Anglian Life*, Abbotts Hall, Stowmarket, Suffolk IP14 1DL. Telephone: 0449 612229.

*Norfolk Rural Life Museum*, Beech House, Gressenhall, East Dereham, Norfolk NR20 4DR. Telephone: 0362 860563.

*Raby Castle*, Staindrop, Darlington, County Durham DL2 3AH. Telephone: 0833 60202.

*Ragley Hall*, Alcester, Warwickshire B49 5NJ. Telephone: 0789 762090.
*Red House Stables*, Old Road, Darley Dale, Derbyshire DE4 2ER. Telephone: 0629 733583.
*The Royal Mews*, Buckingham Palace Road, London SW1W 0QH. Telephone: 071-799 2831.
*Shibden Hall*, Listers Road, Halifax, West Yorkshire HX3 6XG. Telephone: 0422 352246.
*Shugborough*, Milford, Stafford ST17 0XB. Telephone: 0889 881388 extension 211.
*The Shuttleworth Collection*, Old Warden Aerodrome, Biggleswade, Bedfordshire SG18
    9ER. Telephone: 0767 627288.
*Stockwood Craft Museum and Gardens*, Stockwood Country Park, Farley Hill, Luton,
    Bedfordshire LU1 4BH. Telephone: 0582 38714.
*Streetlife – Hull Museum of Transport*, High Street, Hull, North Humberside. Tele-
    phone: 0482 593902.
*Tetley's Brewery Wharf*, The Waterfront, Leeds, West Yorkshire LS1 1QG. Telephone:
    0532 435282.
*Tyrwhitt-Drake Museum of Carriages*, Archbishop's Stables, Mill Street, Maidstone,
    Kent ME15 6YE. Telephone: 0622 754497.
*Ulster Folk and Transport Museum*, Cultra, Holywood, County Down, Northern Ireland
    BT18 0EU. Telephone: 0232 428428.
*Weald and Downland Open Air Museum*, Singleton, Chichester, West Sussex PO18
    0EU. Telephone: 0243 63348.
*York Castle Museum*, Tower Street, York YO1 1RY. Telephone: 0904 653611.
*Yorkshire Museum of Carriages and Horse-drawn Vehicles*, Yore Mill, by Aysgarth
    Falls, Aysgarth, North Yorkshire DL8 3SR. Telephone: 0748 823275.

*Arthur Floyd's idea of bliss: a pleasure drive pure and simple, with dog. The rings, known as
eyes, behind the blinkers take the leader's reins when driving tandem.*